Kensington Fields in 1970.

Several generations of city building seen
in 1966 – looking across Crown Street
toward Entwistle Heights.

# FIRM FOUNDATIONS – THE MAKING OF A CITY

*The face of Liverpool has changed dramatically over the last 200 years, transforming from an industrial port to the bustling and vibrant city we know today...*

When Queen Victoria came to the throne in 1837, Liverpool was a provincial town with a prosperous port.

At the time of her death, 63 years later, the population had more than trebled to some 700,000 and it was widely acclaimed to be the second city of the British Empire.

By 1871 the population had increased dramatically to 493,405 and to 746,421 by 1911. Much of this population growth was due to migration into the city from other parts of Britain, from Ireland, especially after the disastrous famine of 1846-8, and from overseas.

Nineteenth century Liverpool was a city of great contrasts. The fortunate few lived in detached houses with gardens and servants to cook and clean for them.

The unfortunate majority lived in squalid, overcrowded slums.

The city was to show remarkable resilience despite the appalling squalor of the court houses, where the poor lived, died and prayed to their God. Lee Jones, a Victorian philanthropist and founder of the League of Welldoers, provided charitable help in feeding Liverpool's poorest children – he also trained the unflinching lens of his camera on his subjects, providing an astonishing record of the lower echelons of society, as the photographs below show. ➤

## HOPE STREET

These photographs, from the Lee Jones Collection / League of Welldoers, show how children lived in Victorian Liverpool.

➤ As Liverpool's population grew and grew, all these people had to live somewhere – there were a number of different solutions to this problem, some more successful than others.

Thousands of terrace houses were built in Liverpool in the second half of the nineteenth century. The small terrace houses like those in Everton were popular and provided housing for a large proportion of Liverpool's population.

Houses were closely built and a strong sense of community developed.

The city continues to evolve and change – homes have gone up and down – but this sense of community has never been lost.

The steps lovingly cleaned with sandstone by proud housewives on their hands and knees. The old lamp-post that we used to swing around on a rope. Patting the carter's horse or boosting your pocket money by taking empty jam jars to the grocer.

The terraced streets of Scottie Road; the high-rise world of 'the Piggeries'; the self-contained villages of the tenements; the buildings may have long-gone, but the memories remain.

Children gather in Gomer Street, off Queen Anne Street, in 1933.

A court in the Scotland Road area of Liverpool.

Coloured bunting in Grafton Street,
Toxteth Park, June 18, 1957.
Above, tenement blocks on
Melrose Road, opened in 1929.

A striking view from the top of 220ft high Entwistle heights in Harding Street, Toxteth, the city's first 22-storey block of flats. Several Liverpool landmarks old and new are visible in the picture, including the Liver Building, the Littlewoods building, the tower of Liverpool University and construction of the Metropolitan Cathedral, dating the picture to the early 1960s.

## VANISHING POINT

Some would say these terraced rows all look alike, but if you called this street home, then you will probably recognise it as your own.

## SQUARE DEAL

Soho Street (left) was home to tenements known locally as 'Four Squares'.
Above, who'd be a rent man?

Skate expectations for these girls in Kirkby.

Park life – Mrs F Wilson stands at the 'picture window' of her top floor flat in Belem Towers, Sefton Park, 1960.

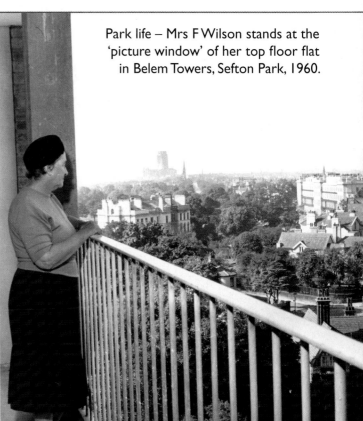

EVERY LITTLE HELPS

Pictured in 1973, this well known landmark on St Oswald Street, Old Swan, is now a Tesco store.

# THE KEAY TO COMMUNITY

*When Lancelot Keay took up the post of Liverpool City Architect in 1925, he had a mammoth task ahead of him...*

The city had twice the housing needs of Manchester, and more slum dwellings than Sheffield, Leeds, and Birmingham.

Housing, he admitted, was "one of the most vital social problems of our time."

In 1933 the Minister of Health asked local authorities for a blueprint for slum clearance.

Keay's response looked up to the task. 5,000 houses were planned for the outskirts of the city, while over 10,000 flats were to be built to accommodate residents from nearby cleared sites.

He managed it and then some, presiding over some 30,000 new homes for people during the inter-war years.

But Keay's vision went further than just providing flats for people.

Just years before construction began on the tenements Keay took a delegation with him to Vienna to see socialist experiments like the Karl Marx Hof. With its long balconies, courtyards, and green spaces, these tenement blocks inspired Keay to build something similar back in Liverpool.

The key was community.

The balconies would encourage more contact between neighbours; the courtyards would act as a meeting area and play area for the kids; and the flats faced inwards so residents could watch out for each other.

Keay's vision was not just an improvement of conditions and facilities. It was about communities that knew each other, looked out for each other, and whose kids could play and feel safe.

Did he succeed? You need only jog the memory of anyone who grew up in Kent Gardens, Caryl Gardens, Gerard Gardens, or any other of Keay's tenements, and the words 'community spirit', 'safety' and 'fun' will more often than not be uttered with fondness and a smile.

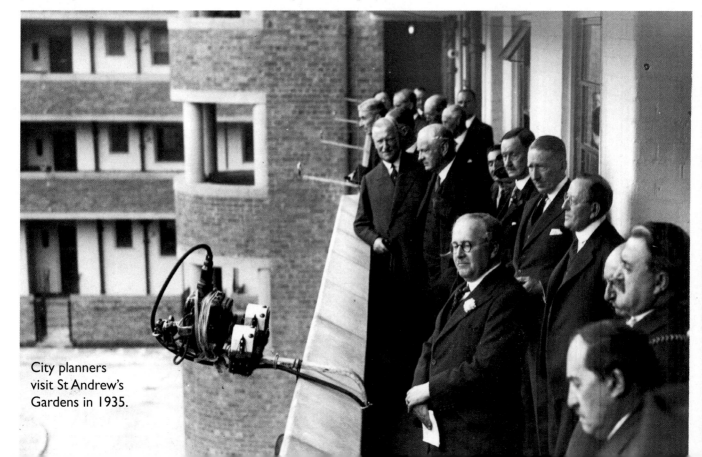

City planners visit St Andrew's Gardens in 1935.

## BRIGHT IDEAS

Municipal sun traps – 'King Gardens' in Mill Street, Toxteth, were designed to give the maximum amount of sunshine, pictured here in 1939. Left, a visit from the High Commissioner of Canada, photographed at the new tenements in Circus Street in 1936, with Lancelot Keay, director of Liverpool Housing.

Myrtle Gardens pictured
in 1955 and opposite page,
exactly a decade on in 1965

Framed by washing are high walls, kids with an old
pram, watched over by mam and nan, dominated
by the Corporation flats in Fontenoy and Byrom
Streets, on their 30th anniversary, in April, 1968.

# CARNIVAL TIME IN THE GOOD OLD DAYS

*Caryl Gardens was an enormous place. With its own youth club, play and sports facilities, shops, bus and even disco nights, you'd be forgiven for thinking it was a self-contained village that just happened to be somewhere near Liverpool...*

But the story of Caryl Gardens matches those of the other Liverpool tenements: strong communities living on top of each other; residents being a part of each other's lives; front doors left open; and neighbours rallying around when help was needed, with the minimum of fuss.

And they had a style of fun all of their own. A direct service to West Kirby, Blackpool, and Rhyl – with onboard refreshments, snacks, and entertainment. No, this is not a first class train service, but the 'Caryly Bus.' And all for 20p!

Staffed by community stalwarts like Roger Draper, the bus was chiefly so that kids could enjoy a day out, leaving early, and returning home by bedtime. The trips were one of the most exciting features of community life for those who could get a seat.

Given to the Southern Neighbourhood Council by the Liverpool Variety Club, it was hoped the ex-Wallasey Corporation bus would "aid community life."

Teddy Gold, then director of the Southern Neighbourhood Council, said: "Neighbourhoods like this need some form of community transport. When people from multi-storey blocks or from streets in the neighbourhood get together to organise a day trip, then friendship must be formed."

Armed with just a white-bread sandwich, a bottle of 'lemo', and a packet of crisps for the whole day, the kids of Caryl Gardens would brim with excitement as the bus made its way.

The packed lunch would usually be gone before they'd even left the city boundaries.

Naturally, the rest of the journey would be taken up by that ubiquitous chant . . .

"We're off! We're off! We're off in a motor car . . ."

In the mid-70s, Caryl Gardens held its carnival parade, with drum majorettes, Snow White and the Seven Dwarfs, streets decorated with flags and bunting, a tug-of-war and even a Miss Southern Neighbourhood competition.

Liverpool FC also owe a debt to those

tenement blocks. Ian Callaghan, Liverpool's most capped player – whose career was the only one to span that of Shankly – grew up kicking a ball about on those squares.

And a certain Robbie Fowler had both sets of grandparents living in the Gardens at one stage. His dad, Bobby, was born there as one of seven, and would have known Ian Callaghan from his school days.

The tenements were built in 1935 and torn down in 1982.

Those that grew up in Caryl Gardens may have been scattered far and wide, but reunions of 300 plus have since sprung up as instantaneously as a 'bommie tower' gathered from scrap wood might have in its day.

## GARDEN PARTY

Above, children at Caryl Gardens in Dingle take part in a sports day run by the Southern Neighbourhood Council in April 1973. The event was organised by local women, and shopkeepers donated the prizes.

## UNDER THE ARCHES

Caryl Gardens pictured in the late 1930s. Built in 1935, the architects obeyed pre-war legislation preventing the "tennies" from being too high. Strong communities lived on top of each other and residents were a part of each other's lives.

# MEMORIES BURN BRIGHT

*Joe Anderson, Liverpool City Council leader,
has a huge pride in his tenement background...*

Joe has powerful memories of being one of six crammed into a bed under a coat in Kent Gardens; collecting coal for his 'mam' and the neighbours; getting toys from the social services for Christmas; taking his uncle's suit to the pawn shop on a Monday and collecting it again on a Friday.

But Joe didn't mind. He lived in a tenement block close to the city centre for 23 years before becoming a councillor for that area.

And he could still tell you the names of every family on those landings.

"We used to know everybody," explained Joe. "They were good times, tough as well, but I wouldn't change them at all. I love keeping in touch with the people from there."

New Year's Eve and the 'Bommie Night' on November 5 always stick in Joe's memory.

He said: "We used to be very tribal, protect each other, collecting scrap wood. We'd have huge big towers. It was that hot it would shatter the windows. We had to be told we couldn't have them that high.

Remember, remember – a bonfire in Myrtle Gardens, in 1979.

"On New Year's the pitch would be chokka. Everybody from all the blocks would come onto the square at midnight. There'd be parties at everyone's house. All the doors would be left open. It was amazing, really amazing. You don't get nights like them anymore."

That would be a release from daily life. And daily life could be hard.

"We had the electricity turned off, the gas turned off, my mum would cook by the stove. We just couldn't afford it. The council used to provide uniforms to the police and fire brigade. If you were a kid whose parents couldn't afford a school uniform you'd get some of the left over clothes and shoes. Even my own married life I found it tough. There was times when I was on the dole. Some people had work and others did not."

And when you haven't got much, whatever help is available is precious.

"I remember at Christmas we got some toys from Social Services. Without that we would have got nothing."

Have those experiences formed his own personal values and motivation?

"Absolutely. The basic principles about supporting people and fairness is still very much underpinning my values and my beliefs and there are examples of that from the tennies. ➤

21

➤ "There was genuine support for one another."

There was a time when tenements were the norm, but some of the characters who lived there were far from it.

Joe remembers living next to one of the most famously unusual residents of Kent Gardens. His name was 'Paddy' Murphy. But he wasn't Irish. His nationality was Japanese.

He came to Liverpool in 1938, as Kanso Yoshida, and soon had to bat off snide comments after Pearl Harbour.

In an interview from the Echo in 1962, he explained in his own way:

"One day I get real mad. And I yell out 'I'm not Japanese, I'm good Englishman as any of you. If you don't like my name, then OK, I change it. Call me Paddy Murphy!' I am known as Paddy Murphy ever since."

Joe recalls: "My dad knew him because they would both go away to sea. Paddy was very quiet and very humble. He used to come into our house on a Saturday afternoon and watch the wrestling.

"Apparently he was related to the Emperor of Japan. He must have been loaded, but he used to show my mum adverts of where butter was a penny different. 'Have you seen this?' he'd say. He had a bus pass so he'd rush off for a bargain on the bus."

And if you thought Paddy was pulling your leg about his royal Japanese links, in 1962, his cousin Princess Chichibu, sister-in-law to Emperor, paid him a visit.

Joe recalls: "They came into the block in their limousine. I'll always remember it. That was something as a kid!"

New flats in Kent Street in June 1954. Right, Princess Chichibu, the Japanese Emperor's sister-in-law, during a visit to the UK in 1967.

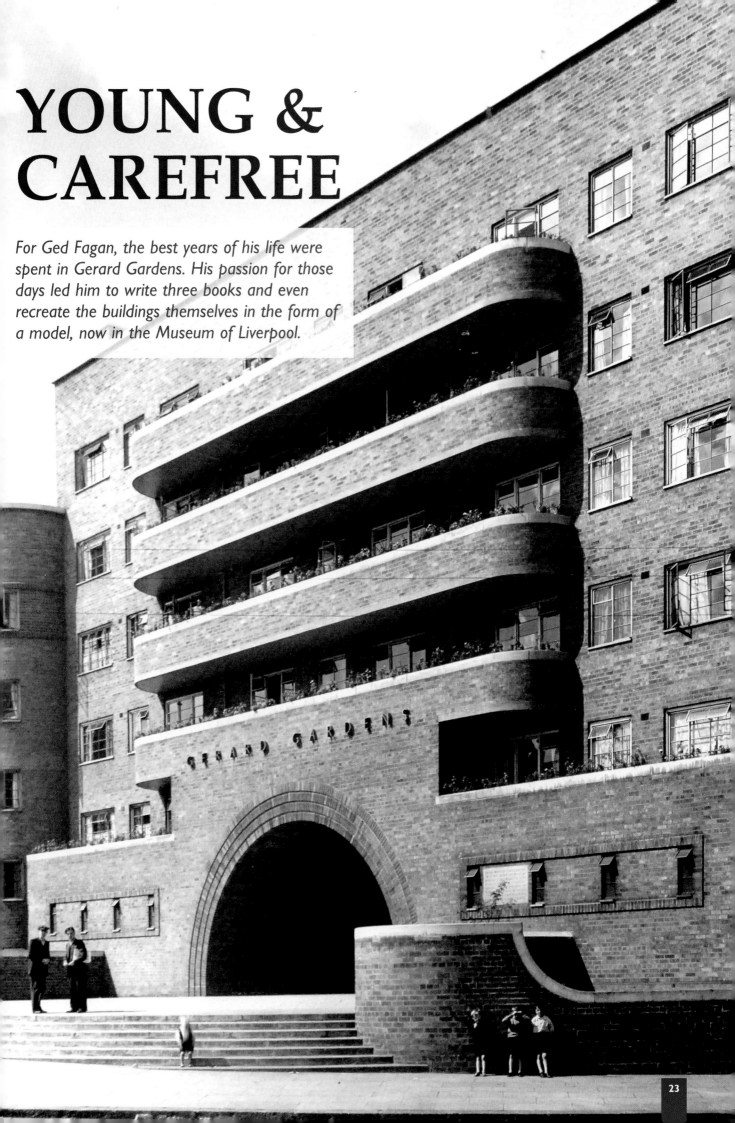

# YOUNG & CAREFREE

For Ged Fagan, the best years of his life were spent in Gerard Gardens. His passion for those days led him to write three books and even recreate the buildings themselves in the form of a model, now in the Museum of Liverpool.

SO what was it about being a kid in Gerard Gardens that gave people such happy memories?

"You always felt safe" says Ged Fagan. "You were young and carefree without any worries. There was poverty but your parents never let you feel it.

"It policed itself. This was around the time when you wouldn't do anything too naughty because it would get back to your mum – they'd all talk to each other about you in the local shops.

"We used to play in St John's Gardens. That was our local place to play around in. We even used to play tick on the steps around Wellington's Column. I'm amazed no one ever broke their neck."

Ged also remembers the perils of playing footy in the tenement courtyards.

He said: "Of course, there'd be no bar so you'd always be arguing over whether it was a goal or not.

"If the footy games weren't on there would be a mass game of kick the can. There was always something going on."

Like many of the tenement squares, the original swings, slides, and roundabouts from the 1930s had been torn down to make way for bomb shelters during the war and were never fully replaced.

"You just had to get on and make your own games," explained Ged.

"One game we used to play in the square was a form of 'Bingo'. Say flats 7a and 7d had their lights on, you'd be waiting for 7b and 7c to go on so you could get a straight line. We were easily amused!"

But all those kids had to go somewhere. Overcrowding was often the biggest problem for families given the inadequately sized flats.

Ged recalls: "I remember families like the Eggers. They had 16 of them sleeping in four bedrooms.

"The lad invited us in one night. In his bedroom there were two sets of bunk beds and a double bed. They had to do the Sunday Roast in 3 lots."

That may have been one extreme, but with families of six, seven, and eight being the norm, the three and four bed flats were often not as spacious as they may have originally seemed to the architects.

Of course, Gerard Gardens weren't the only tenement blocks in the area. Fontenoy Gardens was down the road on Byrom Street, and the tenements known as the Four Squares occupied the

other side of St Anne Street. Those groups gave the kids and teenagers competition.

Ged remembers: "There were friendly rivalries, like bonfire night; different squares nicking the wood and the next night the others going round to get it back. But there were also harsher rivalries with a bit of stone throwing.

"The Four Squares were raised a bit. From Christian Street to St Anne Street there was an incline. So the kids from the Four Squares would have the upper hand because they'd be throwing downwards. But it rarely got too serious.

"That the kids from both sides of the road ended up in the same secondary school meant competition never had much chance of being anything more than another way to kill time in their concrete adventureland."

## FRIENDLY RIVALRIES

Above, the playground in Gerard Gardens. Left, Fontenoy Gardens in 1936. Below, Four Squares in 1935.

# FROM THE BLITZ TO THE BOOM

*After World War II, there was a drastic housing shortage in Britain. Liverpool had been heavily bombed, especially during the blitz of May, 1941. One solution, which at the time was meant to be short term, was prefabricated houses – known everywhere as 'prefabs' – on sites around the city. People wanted a higher standard of living, with the 'luxuries' of a proper bathroom and indoor toilet.*

Pictured top, heroes coming home – but for many there were no homes. Right, mopping up in one of the temporary huts, after cooking with a blowlamp, 1946.

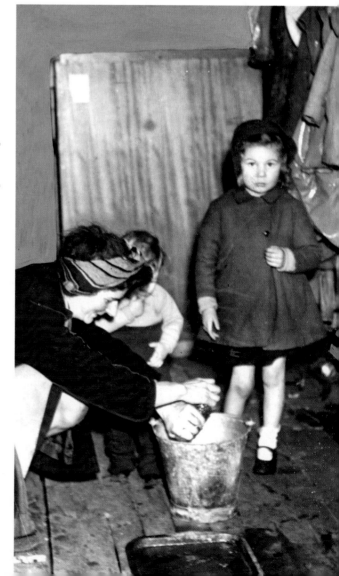

Alongside old tenement blocks in Prince Edwin Street, a colony of Liverpool's instant homes springs up in 1964. 28 dwellings occupied the derelict bombed site.

Mr and Mrs McHugh enjoy a cup of tea at the West Derby army camp, 1946.

## MAKE AND MEND

Mrs Matelot, the wife of a Free French naval rating, with her son Francis, who moved into one of the disused army huts off Leyfield Road, West Derby, 1940. Below left, cleaning up the hut at the army camp at Town Row, West Derby in readiness for a family to move in, in 1946. Right, pre-fab homes built in 1945 by the Ministry of Works at Townsend Avenue, Liverpool. Built-in cupboards, sink, a washboiler, cooker and refrigerator were provided.

## WEDDING VOWS

Touring the streets of Liverpool in 1950, the bride and bridegroom have their furniture with them and the placard asks: "Where's that house, Mr Bevan?"

## PROMISED LAND

Ten pound poms – setting sail for pastures new, emigrants start the first of the new friendships they will make on the voyage from Liverpool to Sydney in 1949.

The Lord Mayor of Liverpool opens the first of the new permanent houses at Chelwood Avenue, Broadgreen, in August 1946.

## GOLDEN AGE

Left, a crowd gather outside an exhibition house on Aber Street in 1955. Above, Mr and Mrs Lloyd at the smokeless solid fuel burner in the kitchen of their Aber Street home. Below, living the dream with all the mod-cons in the 1950s.

# POOR IN POCKET, RICH IN SPIRIT

*After the Second World War, the older housing stock began to degenerate into 'slum' conditions. There was poverty but your parents never let you feel it...*

The Nelson family make the best of their situation in 1968.

THE HOUSING A...

CITY OF LIVER...
(MENZIES STREET
COMPULSORY PURCHASE

WHEREAS the Council
Liverpool have submitted to...
Housing and Local Government
the above-named order whic...
them to acquire compulsorily...
of Part III of the Housing Act...
clearance areas, the land inclu...

NOTICE IS HEREBY G...
Public Local Inquiry into this...
held by J. A. Martin, Esq...
(Edin.), Architect, at the Mun...
Dale Street, Liverpool, 2...
13th May, 1969, commencing...

A copy of the order an...
referred to therein are on depos...
Clerk's Office, Development Secre...
House, 13 17 Sir Thomas Stree...
and may be seen there, on an...
reasonable hours.

S. F...
Authorised...
of Housing...
to...
5th MARCH, 1969.

GIVE DECENT HOMES FOR US & OUR CHILDREN.

## SIGN OF THE TIMES

Above, the sign of the Compulsory Purchase Order can mean many things, 1969.
Left, graffiti declares "Give decent homes for us and our children".

## HARD TIMES

Top, a kitchen sink drama for Mrs Wilde, pictured in her kitchen in 1974. Left, a woman's work is never done – 1960.

## ORDINARY WORLD

Pictured top, Rev Brian Green, Rev Donald May and Father Edmund Whitaker visit Joliffe Street, off North Hill Street, near Princes Park, after concern among residents over housing conditions, 1962. Above, mealtime for everybody in this Everton home in 1962.

The view from the top of Pendine Close in Sheil Park in 1967, as the construction of a 22-storey block begins to dominate the skyline.

# THE SKY'S THE LIMIT

*As the terraced houses fell into disrepair, land available for new building was in short supply. The architects looked up for inspiration. Work started on Liverpool's first high-rise block of flats in 1953 – 'Coronation Court' in Fazakerley was opened in 1956. Multi-storey flats seemed to be the answer to the city's housing problem and offered a whole new view on the world.*

Twilight falls on Coronation Court in 1956. Left, the grand opening earlier that year.

Flats in Sefton
Park, 1966.

# ON TOP OF THE WORLD

*High-rise heaven or high-rise hell? Memories of Everton's homes in the sky . . .*

JOHN Hutchinson was raised in Cambridge, but you could say he had his real education in Everton.

John moved to the area in 1971, a fresh-faced 21 year old. These days a student might have a gap year planting trees in a jungle, or teaching English in the mountains of Peru. Back then, John and his wife, Hilary, scaled a different heights altogether – Brynford Heights on Conway Street in Everton. With more high-rises than any other area in the country, you'd be foolish to think it wasn't as much of a culture shock.

John recalls: "We were hippies back then, with just a mattress on the floor, but we only had one gas fire for the whole flat. It was absolutely freezing!

"It was exciting for us. We made a lovely home at the top of that tower block. You could walk

around the whole balcony. The views were fantastic."

John had come to Everton to volunteer in a local youth club, Shrewsbury House. He remembers his first evening there:

"One of the older kids got hold of me by the neck and said 'What's

a divvy?' – that was the first thing he said to me! I said 'I don't know'. He said, 'You are.'"

In typical Liverpool fashion, that same teenager took John under his wing, showed him the area and gave him credibility with the other youngsters – all within just a few days of meeting him.

"I was drawn into the place very quickly. I immediately felt part of it. It was intimidating, but it was also welcoming, full of life, boisterous and warm. I just thought 'wow, this is exciting!'."

But just as John was getting the hang of high-rise Everton, Everton was falling out of love with high-rises:

"By the early 70s, there were significant problems emerging with the tower blocks. It always started with small things like smells in the lifts, graffiti on the walls. ➤

High-rise flats on
Garibaldi Street in 1960.

➤ "If that goes on all the time,
mothers with toddlers and prams
will eventually be telling their
husbands 'we've got to move'.

"The more families move out,
the less suitable the blocks become
for the remaining families and the
more likely you are to get a burglar
moving in on your landing."

John ended up working
permanently at Shrewsbury House
and moved into a house right next
to the youth club with his wife
Hilary and young family.

But like many other Everton
families who witnessed the blocks
tumbling down around them like
giant dominoes, they made a new
home for themselves away from
the rubble. Except John's high-rise
story didn't end there.

In his determination to make his
old home, now in Everton Park,
a place people will visit again, he
and an army of volunteers, have

been planting fruit trees, vegetables
and flowers up and down the
park's slopes.

If you look close enough, you'll
find a secret orchard, bearing fruit,
right where one of those colossal
tower blocks once stood.

Peter Brennan is better placed
than most when it comes to talking
about troubles in the tower blocks.

It wasn't because he was a
suffering resident, but because
he was one of those kids who'd
cause mayhem: Going up and
down the lifts; knocking on doors;
and stealing 'freebies' that well-
meaning salespeople stuck through
letterboxes.

Peter's grandmother lived in
Mazzini Heights on Roscommon
Street, where he'd visit her
regularly.

He said: "We loved going there
because it was so high up.

"My aunt was a stewardess on

the liners. The arrival times of the
ships would be in the Echo, so we
could see her ship coming into
the Mersey from the tenth floor in
Mazzini. As soon as we'd see it we
would run down to the Pier Head
to find out what presents she'd
brought back for us."

When you were passing the time
as a kid surrounded by concrete
with nowhere to play, creativity
and mischief were the name of the
game.

Peter recalls: "We used to tie
string between the door knocker
and the railing on the balcony.
Then we'd bang on the door and
run away. When people opened
it, they'd have to yank the door
and the door knocker would come
flying off."

You may remember those
little samples of chocolate and
toothpaste you would sometimes
get through your letterboxes. That

March of progress through a broken window, a net fringe flutters in a shattered window, framing tower blocks of flats sprouting on the spot where streets of two up and two down houses once slanted up towards Netherfield Road – 1967.

is, unless you lived in Mazzini Heights, in which case you may have been at the mercy of Peter and his mates stealing them all. He remembers:

"These women with bags would stick Toblerones through people's doors. We'd follow them round from one floor to the next taking out all the ones that stuck out the letterboxes. I can't even eat Toblerones, but we'd take them all down to the shop and exchange them for something else."

With all that trouble, you would have thought it was a nightmare living in the tower blocks. Of course, for many it was, though for far more pressing reasons than

door knockers and samples of toothpaste going missing.

Equally some loved their homes in the sky. Peter's grandmother was definitely of the latter category.

He said: "She moved from the terraced streets. So for the first time in her life she had hot running water, an indoor toilet and a bath! She still had contact with her relatives and old neighbours, because they moved into Mazzini Heights too."

But there was one little snag – central heating:

"She could never get used to it, so she had it disconnected," explained Peter. "Not because the

bills were high, but just because she didn't understand it. It was underfloor and she'd walk around on a warm floor and say 'ooo no, I can't have that'. So she bought an electric heater with a coal effect and orange ribbons that danced like flames instead."

Decades later, she moved into a new build bungalow in West Derby, with better facilities, a garden and zero trouble.

But for a woman who'd lived in her street in the sky for 23 years, it was something of a fall from grace.

"She hated it, from the day she moved in to the day she died," recalls Peter. "People weren't the same she used to say."

# WHAT GOES UP...

"You wouldn't get me up in one of these."
The opening of Valley View Flats in
Childwall in 1964 (now demolished).

Olive Mount, Wavertree takes shape in
1962, viewed from Wellstead Road.

Thirty years of tears, joy and tragedy come crashing down in nine seconds, when five blocks of flats nicknamed the ugly sisters of Lee Park came down in 1992. The five blocks, a landmark on the South Liverpool skyline and visible for miles, were built in the 1960s.

# ...MUST COME DOWN!

# THE KIDS ARE ALRIGHT . . .

Two youngsters try out the new slide in the playground of Canterbury Heights in 1966.

## PLAY TIME

Above, children gather outside Gerard Gardens having great fun in front of the camera.
Left, the health and safety brigade would never allow it today. Children at play in the rubble off Netherfield Road, July 1964.

## ROUGH AND TUMBLE

Above, the prize-winning development of Damerham Croft, Belle Vale – but in 1973 there were complaints about damp from residents. The kids didn't seem to mind too much. Left, an adventure on the igloo climbing frame on the Netherley Estate.

Children from Childwall Heights at play.

Children swing on the balcony rails of Haigh Heights, 1966.

Jacqueline Hulse and her brother Joseph look out over Sefton Park in 1970. Their mother, Edna Hulse, told the Liverpool Echo: "I've had my fears of the kids falling off the balconies or down the stairs."

Running down a
dream in 1973.

# THE WASTELANDS

*In 1960, as The Beatles prepared us for a musical revolution that would rock the world, another event was unfolding in the heart of the city that would lead to an exodus of biblical proportions. Over 100,000 people began to leave the spiritual homes of their forefathers, bulldozed into the suburbs in the name of progress and slum clearance. The city's skyline across its most visible and historic inner city districts – notably Everton and Scotland Road – would never be the same again.*

Above, 31 years after the end of the Second World War and the Anglican Cathedral still has that bombed look about it in 1976 – but the scene was about to change as the old buildings in Great George Street were demolished giving the Cathedral a more worthy setting.

## GHOST TOWN

Above, living among the bricks
and rubble, in the wake of the
bulldozer, 1970.

## TREAD CAREFULLY

Left, Mrs Elizabeth Dickson
crosses derelict land near
Spencer Street to go
shopping in 1969.

## LOST IN THE DESERT

And not even a drop of water.

Beatrice Romney and her daughter Karen look out from their home at Milburn Heights, Everton, in 1967.

Catching up on street gossip — at least the neighbours won't hear — 1974.

## MEMORY LANE

"I used to live up there".

# MY KIND OF TOWN

The ups and downs of high-rise living were not for everybody – once again the long-suffering communities were broken up to the four corners of Merseyside. New towns, such as Kirkby, Runcorn and Skelmersdale were set up, built on what was previously farm land.

## IN THE MIX

Children play on a cement mixer in Skelmersdale in the 1960s.
Left, a 'see-for-yourself' tour of houses in Skelmersdale in 1968.

## DOWN ON THE FARM

Top, a fashion-conscious family in Cantril Farm, 1966. Left, residents of the Netherley Estate use their mobile shop, 1968. Above, a quiet summer's day in Croxteth, August 1982.

The promise of a sunny future in Kirkby.

Left, tranquil Kirkby pictured just before the Second World War in 1939, and below, houses on the Southdene portion of Kirkby, 1957.

Kirkby flats demolished in 1982 – the seven-storey blocks of Tower Hill maisonettes, built just twelve years before, were still to be paid for over many decades. The 600 homes, which were never fully occupied, were blown up with a series of controlled detonations over three weekends.

They promised a bright future in Southgate, Runcorn. The multi-coloured development was nicknamed 'Legoland'.

Wind of change – Speke in 1973

Speke was planned in 1936 as a complete town for 22,000 people, living in 5,700 houses and flats. Unfortunately building work was interupted by World War II and not completed until 1957. At one point Speke was the second largest housing estate in western Europe with over 35,000 people jammed into less than 5,000 homes. This image shows work on a quadrant of flats near the Civic Centre, and right, houses on a Liverpool Corporation Estate in Sherdley Walk in 1958.

Speke Road Gardens
(and above) in 1933

*High-rise flats and housing estates were built to accommodate families that wanted to escape overcrowded housing, but many became concrete jungles, blighted by decline – bleak, suffocated and soulless.*

Treading the hallways of a high-rise in Netherley, 1979.

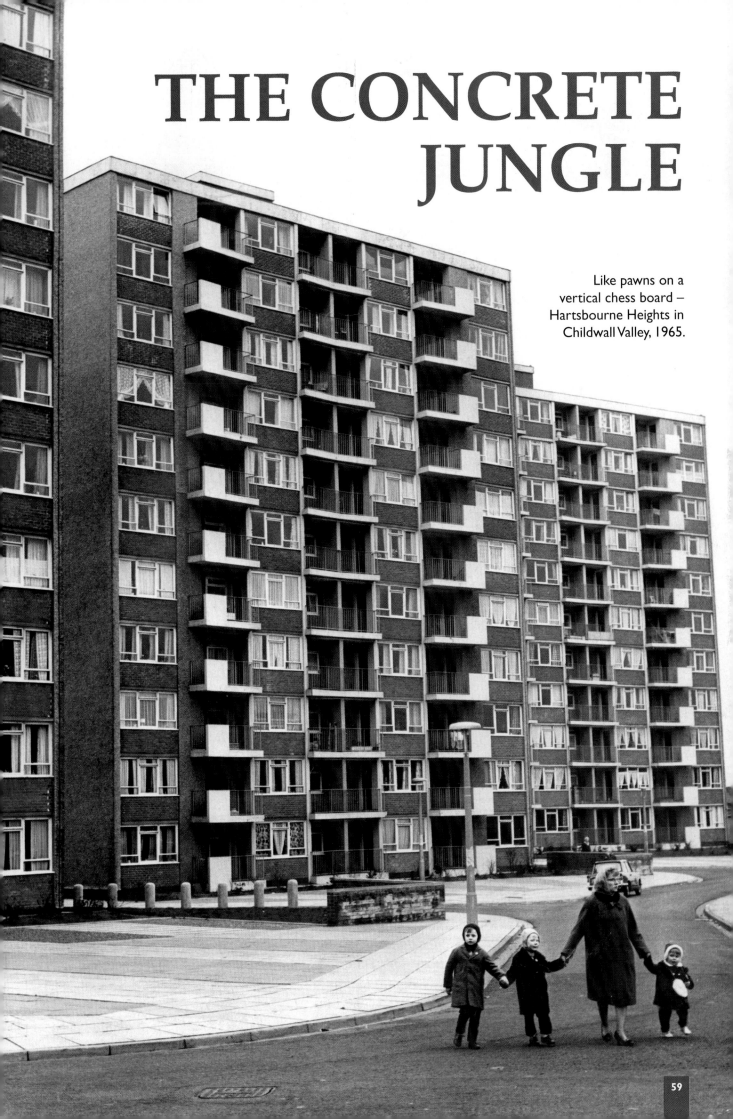

# THE CONCRETE JUNGLE

Like pawns on a vertical chess board – Hartsbourne Heights in Childwall Valley, 1965.

## PARADISE LOST?

In the 1960s you could enjoy long, country walks in Netherley. Above, the Wood Lane area in 1989. Left, Peckmill Green in 1979.

## I'M STILL STANDING

Below, new homes for old – a family with three young children were still living in this house in Liverpool's Leander Street in 1963.

How long will it look good? Spick and span from the builder's hands come new council flats in Robertson Street, Dingle, 1961.

Grass through the pavements – boarded up houses, it wasn't meant to be like this. The Boundary Street area in 1990.

# CARING FOR THE OLD FOLKS

Main picture, Mrs Lee in her kitchen in Mill Lane, Broadgreen, and in her new kitchen – December 17, 1987.

Better conditions for old people – washing up with modern facilities, at home in Bailey House, Queens Drive, 1959.

## YOUNG AT HEART

Lucy Fisher in her 'modernised kitchenette', in 1967.
Right, Mr and Mrs Gadd have a restful afternoon at Broomfield Green, Sefton Park, in 1961.

TORONTO·CLOSE
THESE·TWENTY·FLATS·FOR·AGED·PERSONS·WHO·SU
THE·BOMBING·OF·MERSEYSIDE·WERE·BUILT·BY
A·GRANT·FROM·THE·NATIONAL·AIR·RAID·D
FUND·OF·THE·LORD·MAYOR·OF·LONDON·TH
NAMED·AFTER·THE·CITY·OF·TORONTO
DOMINION·OF·CANADA·TO·COMMEMO
CONTRIBUTIONS·OF·THE·COMMONWEALTH
OPENED·ON·BEHALF·OF·THE·COUNTY
BIRKENHEAD·BOOTLE·LIVERPOOL·AN
SIR·GEORGE·WILKINSON·BARONET
LONDON·1940-1941·ON·THE

## FIRM FOUNDATIONS

Above, a memorial stone unveiled by
Sir George H Wilkinson at the 20 flats
for elderly people at the junction of
Stockbridge Lane and Knowsley Lane,
Huyton, in 1952. The residences for old
people who lost their homes through
enemy action, were erected by the City
Housing Committee.

# BLISS IN THE PROMISED LAND

Ann Webster in her new home in 1977.

*In 1977, the dreams of four friends and neighbours became reality, as the Holy Land Housing Cooperative handed them the keys to their new front doors...*

The 'Holy Land' neighbourhood of Liverpool's Dingle area, was now the 'Promised Land' for more than 100 residents who had been waiting to see their dreams of better housing conditions come true.

The move was the first small beginning of a decanting scheme to give Dingle residents a chance of better homes without breaking up the community spirit – a problem faced by slum clearance programmes.

Instead, the Housing Association bought 106 houses in the David Street, Isaac Street, Jacob Street and Moses Street area. Their Biblical names give the area its 'Holy Land'.

Until 1974 the houses had been owned by one private landlord's estate and came on the market after the estate 'broke'. With capital provided by the Government's Housing Corporation, the association bought the three-bedroomed type terraced homes. Average price paid for the homes was £1,300 and another £5,000 modernisation was to be spent on each. The tenants joined the cooperative by purchasing a £1 share.

Gone were the outdoor toilets and scullery kitchens, replaced by architect-designed extensions.

One of the lucky residents was Ann Webster of Jacob Street, who moved from her home of 41 years, where she raised four children, to next-door with its modern facilities.

"The only thing I will miss is my coal fire," she reflected.

A celebration at Dingle House, Dingle Mount, in the 1970s.

The 'bizzies' get busy at Dingle Mount, in 1959.

Toasting their move en masse in 1988, this close-knit community swopped now-demolished Dingle House (pictured inset) for new hope in Shorefields Village. In 1981 they decided they had to get away from their crumbling homes. They formed a housing cooperative and in 1986, finally got what they wanted - a plot of land off Dingle Road on the International Garden Festival site. Joyce Hewitt, secretary of Shorefields housing cooperative, said: "Dingle House was just disgusting. At times it felt like we were up against a brick wall, but we were never tempted to give up."

# THE SHAME OF THE SLUMS IN THE SKY

*Unloved and unmourned – Haigh, Canterbury and Crosbie Heights, 1965-1987...*

Once Liverpool's most notorious slum, the Piggeries in Everton – dubbed 'slums in the sky' – were brought down to earth brick by brick. It signalled the end of a 21-year headache which saw the planners' version of the high-life, crumble in a heap.

The flats were built in 1965 as the answer to Liverpool's housing problems. Families were promised a new lease of life, high above the decaying inner city. It should have brought happiness for hundreds, but instead brought only misery.

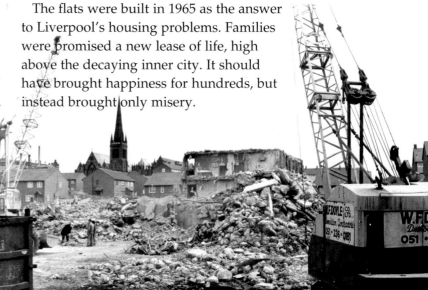

Pat Glover, and her sister Jacqueline, enjoy the view from Canterbury Heights with their aunt in 1966.

The 'intolerable' height of the Piggeries, seen in 1977, taken by Liverpool Echo photographer Stephen Shakeshaft.

# MY BEAUTIFUL LAUNDERETTE

*The wash houses meant a complete break-away from the days when women had to struggle with loads of washing to the public laundries.*

## SQUEAKY CLEAN

The washing line, city style, and a happy smile from this line of satisfied customers at the new Vauxhall civic laundry which was officially opened in Vauxhall Road, Liverpool, 1969.

The official opening was made by Alderman Meadows, former chairman of the Baths and Public Laundries Committee, who unveiled a commemorative plaque. Costing £16,000, the new laundry was the first, fully-automatic coin-operated laundry to be built by Liverpool Corporation. Gone were the days of carrying loads of washing to the Burroughs Gardens laundry, or the old public laundry in Clare Street, which the new one replaced.

## WASH YOUR TROUBLES AWAY

Above, regulars at Burroughs Gardens wash house, 1970.

## SOAP OPERA

The battling Fred Robinson wash-house women declared war on the city council in December 1986, after an uneasy three-month truce. For three weeks, women who used Liverpool's last public wash-house in St Domingo Road, Everton, barricaded themselves inside the building in protest at a decision to shut the place down.

## SPIN CITY

Above, Mrs Eileen McDonald has a washing machine but, with ten people to wash for, she is still forced to carry heavy bundles of clothes across a busy road to the launderette – 1974. Right, Mrs Purcell enjoys a joke with one of the regulars at the wash-house in 1970. Below, Pounding away at the weekly wash in the 1960s.

Tony McGann and Eldon Street residents on the site of their new cooperative in 1986.

# HOME IS WHERE THE HEART IS

*It would be easy to look at the degradation, the demolition and the dodgy reputations given to the 1930s tenement experiments, and think "Good riddance"...*

But that would ignore the success stories of the blocks that were saved, like the Bullring and Myrtle Gardens, that still have an indisputable grace and charm about them.

More glaringly, it ignores the testimony of those who actually lived there.

Tony McGann should know as much as anyone. He set up the famous Eldonian Village in order to keep people from being scattered to the four corners, like so many of the other tenement communities:

Tony said: "The people in the tenement blocks were very happy.

"I think what really made it special was that you could stand outside your home, look out, and there were always people around talking. Everyone knew one another.

"And they kept those tenement blocks beautiful. They took pride in them. To this day quite a few of them could have stayed there. A lot of people cried, even when they were coming over here to the new Eldonian properties."

Tony grew up in Gildarts Gardens.

He saw those blocks, and the shops and businesses they supported, get flushed down the Kingsway Tunnel entrance in the 1970s.

When he subsequently moved into Burlington Street, he was

determined not to see the same thing happen again.

But did the tenants want to see their blocks saved?

"Not when you've got young kids and you're up five-stories high," he explained.

Today the Eldonian Village is an array of beautiful homes, canals and gardens.

Tony said: "You certainly don't have to push prams up any stairs there. It was as simple as the tenants wanting to stick together, and stay nearby.

"It's easy to break a community up, but it's a lot harder to make a community as well. "

Maybe that's why they call it community spirit.

Making their own fun at Melrose Road – the two captains kick off for the start of the cup final between Shamrock Rovers and the Hippy Hipsters.

## STREET LIFE

It's not the homes, it's the people that make the city. Two images of Cawdor Street show generations of change. Left, three lads entertain the photographer in 1973, and right, May Gregory outside her home, pictured in 1994.

## ALL PULL TOGETHER

Real community spirit captured by the Netherley Carnival in 1977. Organised and paid for by the people who live in Netherley, a week-long programme of events was arranged to interest all ages.

Children of Cambridge Street, Wavertree, empty the old folks' bins during a refuse strike in the 1970s.

Down on the farm – youngsters in the Inner City farmyard near Canning Street, Liverpool 8, 1981.

## PAINT THE TOWN

A huge painting of the Madonna and Child outside a house in High Park Street, Toxteth. Artist David Vaughan put his painting on the side of the Rathbone Project's headquarters in September 1976 - the painting was used originally by local children as a backdrop for a film.

# TENEMENT BLOCKS

*By Bobby Parry*

The Tenement blocks came tumbling down, reduced to concrete dust,
The heart and soul of my old town, was ripped and left to rust.
An empire lost to sad neglect, with writing on the wall,
By men who chose to self elect, high rise became our fall.

A sad demise was wearing thin, the people stood and cried,
As glass was soon replaced by tin, the cuts were deep and wide.
The friendly folk of Scotland Road, were breaking at the seam,
With lost tribes losing their abode, no longer as a team.

The Bullring was a saving grace, but Gerard lost his way,
His gardens were so out of place, its crescent in dismay.
Vauxhall went with Fontenoy, whilst Blackstock sealed its fate,
Old Portland went with Thomas White, a drive to desecrate.

The slaughterhouse was out to please, the suits in London town,
With three of them called piggeries, together crashing down.
Our history was being made, but in a dreadful way,
The places where I often played, were left to just decay.

The ball of steel was often feared, to knock us off our block,
The legs of man just disappeared, like fingers on The Clock.
The pubs that served us well were doomed, last orders calling time,
The death knell came as sadness loomed, this cleansing was a crime.

The Braddock's were another jewel, bereft of any crown,
A gem whose fate was also cruel, these flats were part of town.
Woodstock, Hopwood, Ashfield too, with many more to name,
Great people from this chosen crew, were born and bred for fame.

The four squares stood for what was home, these tenements were great,
Our colony was built like Rome, like heaven's golden gate.
So open wide and reminisce, I'm sorry if I erred,
Not naming all is such a miss, but otherwise I cared.

For each and every block in town, that made this city proud,
I named the one's I hung around, but we are all one crowd.
We all belong to Liverpool, our flats were there to nest,
To raise our kids in our old school, is just the perfect crest.

Now I am just a Gardenite, I'm proud that I am here,
My mother's care will shine so bright, forever in my tear.
To keep our dreams alive is great, remember as I cry,
The words I give to you my mate, is finished with goodbye.

The changing face of Liverpool, illustrated by this picture of the new multi-storey blocks of flats going up in the Vauxhall Road area of Liverpool, 1960.

## HERE I STAND

The tenements may have had their challenges, but they made people feel as if they belonged to a community, where it was all for one and one for all – where you were proud to say: "This is my home".

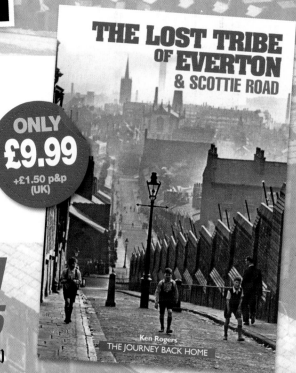